Recipe:

Serving:

Prep Time:

Cook Time:

Temperature:

Ingredients:

Methods:

Wine Pairing:

From the Kitchen of:

Wine Name

Winery Region

Grapes Vintage Alcohol %

Appearance		☆ ☆ ☆ ☆ ☆
Aroma		☆ ☆ ☆ ☆ ☆
Body		☆ ☆ ☆ ☆ ☆
Taste		☆ ☆ ☆ ☆ ☆
Finish		☆ ☆ ☆ ☆ ☆

Pairs With	Serving Temperature

Notes

Ratings ☆ ☆ ☆ ☆ ☆

Recipe:

Serving:

Prep Time:

Cook Time:

Temperature:

Ingredients:

Methods:

Wine Pairing:

From the Kitchen of:

Wine Name

Winery

Region

Grapes

Vintage

Alcohol %

Appearance		☆ ☆ ☆ ☆ ☆
Aroma		☆ ☆ ☆ ☆ ☆
Body		☆ ☆ ☆ ☆ ☆
Taste		☆ ☆ ☆ ☆ ☆
Finish		☆ ☆ ☆ ☆ ☆

Pairs With

Serving Temperature

Notes

Ratings ☆ ☆ ☆ ☆ ☆

Recipe:

Serving:

Prep Time:

Cook Time:

Temperature:

Ingredients:

Methods:

Wine Pairing:

From the Kitchen of:

Wine Name

Winery ______ Region ______

Grapes ______ Vintage ______ Alcohol % ______

Appearance		☆ ☆ ☆ ☆ ☆
Aroma		☆ ☆ ☆ ☆ ☆
Body		☆ ☆ ☆ ☆ ☆
Taste		☆ ☆ ☆ ☆ ☆
Finish		☆ ☆ ☆ ☆ ☆

Pairs With	Serving Temperature

Notes

Ratings ☆ ☆ ☆ ☆ ☆

Recipe:

Serving:

Prep Time:

Cook Time:

Temperature:

Ingredients:

Methods:

Wine Pairing:

From the Kitchen of:

Wine Name ______________________

Winery ______________ Region ______________

Grapes ______________ Vintage ______________ Alcohol % ________

Appearance		☆ ☆ ☆ ☆ ☆
Aroma		☆ ☆ ☆ ☆ ☆
Body		☆ ☆ ☆ ☆ ☆
Taste		☆ ☆ ☆ ☆ ☆
Finish		☆ ☆ ☆ ☆ ☆

Pairs With	Serving Temperature

Notes

Ratings ☆ ☆ ☆ ☆ ☆

Recipe:

Serving:

Prep Time:

Cook Time:

Temperature:

Ingredients:

Methods:

Wine Pairing:

From the Kitchen of:

Wine Name ____________________

Winery ____________ Region ____________

Grapes ____________ Vintage ____________ Alcohol % ________

Appearance		☆ ☆ ☆ ☆ ☆
Aroma		☆ ☆ ☆ ☆ ☆
Body		☆ ☆ ☆ ☆ ☆
Taste		☆ ☆ ☆ ☆ ☆
Finish		☆ ☆ ☆ ☆ ☆

Pairs With	Serving Temperature

Notes

Ratings ☆ ☆ ☆ ☆ ☆

Recipe:

Serving:

Prep Time:

Cook Time:

Temperature:

Ingredients:

Methods:

Wine Pairing:

From the Kitchen of:

Wine Name

Winery ______________ Region ______________

Grapes ______________ Vintage ______________ Alcohol % ______________

Appearance		☆ ☆ ☆ ☆ ☆
Aroma		☆ ☆ ☆ ☆ ☆
Body		☆ ☆ ☆ ☆ ☆
Taste		☆ ☆ ☆ ☆ ☆
Finish		☆ ☆ ☆ ☆ ☆

Pairs With	Serving Temperature

Notes

Ratings ☆ ☆ ☆ ☆ ☆

Recipe:

Serving:

Prep Time:

Cook Time:

Temperature:

Ingredients:

Methods:

Wine Pairing:

From the Kitchen of:

Wine Name

Winery | Region

Grapes | Vintage | Alcohol %

Appearance		☆ ☆ ☆ ☆ ☆
Aroma		☆ ☆ ☆ ☆ ☆
Body		☆ ☆ ☆ ☆ ☆
Taste		☆ ☆ ☆ ☆ ☆
Finish		☆ ☆ ☆ ☆ ☆

Pairs With

Serving Temperature

Notes

Ratings ☆ ☆ ☆ ☆ ☆

Recipe:

Serving:

Prep Time:

Cook Time:

Temperature:

Ingredients:

Methods:

Wine Pairing:

From the Kitchen of:

Wine Name

Winery Region

Grapes Vintage Alcohol %

Appearance		☆ ☆ ☆ ☆ ☆
Aroma		☆ ☆ ☆ ☆ ☆
Body		☆ ☆ ☆ ☆ ☆
Taste		☆ ☆ ☆ ☆ ☆
Finish		☆ ☆ ☆ ☆ ☆

Pairs With	Serving Temperature

Notes

Ratings ☆ ☆ ☆ ☆ ☆

Recipe:

Serving:

Prep Time:

Cook Time:

Temperature:

Ingredients:

Methods:

Wine Pairing:

From the Kitchen of:

Wine Name ____________________

Winery ______________ Region ______________

Grapes ______________ Vintage ______________ Alcohol % __________

Appearance		☆ ☆ ☆ ☆ ☆
Aroma		☆ ☆ ☆ ☆ ☆
Body		☆ ☆ ☆ ☆ ☆
Taste		☆ ☆ ☆ ☆ ☆
Finish		☆ ☆ ☆ ☆ ☆

Pairs With	Serving Temperature

Notes

Ratings ☆ ☆ ☆ ☆ ☆

Recipe:

Serving:

Prep Time:

Cook Time:

Temperature:

Ingredients:

Methods:

Wine Pairing:

From the Kitchen of:

Wine Name

Winery Region

Grapes Vintage Alcohol %

Appearance		☆ ☆ ☆ ☆ ☆
Aroma		☆ ☆ ☆ ☆ ☆
Body		☆ ☆ ☆ ☆ ☆
Taste		☆ ☆ ☆ ☆ ☆
Finish		☆ ☆ ☆ ☆ ☆

Pairs With	Serving Temperature

Notes

Ratings ☆ ☆ ☆ ☆ ☆

Recipe:

Serving:

Prep Time:

Cook Time:

Temperature:

Ingredients:

Methods:

Wine Pairing:

From the Kitchen of:

Wine Name ______________________

Winery ____________ Region ____________

Grapes ____________ Vintage ____________ Alcohol % ________

Appearance		☆ ☆ ☆ ☆ ☆
Aroma		☆ ☆ ☆ ☆ ☆
Body		☆ ☆ ☆ ☆ ☆
Taste		☆ ☆ ☆ ☆ ☆
Finish		☆ ☆ ☆ ☆ ☆

Pairs With	Serving Temperature

Notes

Ratings ☆ ☆ ☆ ☆ ☆

Recipe:

Serving:

Prep Time:

Cook Time:

Temperature:

Ingredients:

Methods:

Wine Pairing:

From the Kitchen of:

Wine Name

Winery ______ Region ______

Grapes ______ Vintage ______ Alcohol % ______

Appearance		☆ ☆ ☆ ☆ ☆
Aroma		☆ ☆ ☆ ☆ ☆
Body		☆ ☆ ☆ ☆ ☆
Taste		☆ ☆ ☆ ☆ ☆
Finish		☆ ☆ ☆ ☆ ☆

Pairs With	Serving Temperature

Notes

Ratings ☆ ☆ ☆ ☆ ☆

Recipe:

Serving:

Prep Time:

Cook Time:

Temperature:

Ingredients:

Methods:

Wine Pairing:

From the Kitchen of:

Wine Name

Winery | Region

Grapes | Vintage | Alcohol %

Appearance		☆ ☆ ☆ ☆ ☆
Aroma		☆ ☆ ☆ ☆ ☆
Body		☆ ☆ ☆ ☆ ☆
Taste		☆ ☆ ☆ ☆ ☆
Finish		☆ ☆ ☆ ☆ ☆

Pairs With	Serving Temperature

Notes

Ratings ☆ ☆ ☆ ☆ ☆

Recipe:

Serving:

Prep Time:

Cook Time:

Temperature:

Ingredients:

Methods:

Wine Pairing:

From the Kitchen of:

Wine Name

Winery ____________ Region ____________

Grapes ____________ Vintage ____________ Alcohol % ____________

Appearance		☆ ☆ ☆ ☆ ☆
Aroma		☆ ☆ ☆ ☆ ☆
Body		☆ ☆ ☆ ☆ ☆
Taste		☆ ☆ ☆ ☆ ☆
Finish		☆ ☆ ☆ ☆ ☆

Pairs With	Serving Temperature

Notes

Ratings ☆ ☆ ☆ ☆ ☆

Recipe:

Serving:

Prep Time:

Cook Time:

Temperature:

Ingredients:

Methods:

Wine Pairing:

From the Kitchen of:

Wine Name

Winery   Region

Grapes   Vintage   Alcohol %

Appearance		☆ ☆ ☆ ☆ ☆
Aroma		☆ ☆ ☆ ☆ ☆
Body		☆ ☆ ☆ ☆ ☆
Taste		☆ ☆ ☆ ☆ ☆
Finish		☆ ☆ ☆ ☆ ☆

Pairs With

Serving Temperature

Notes

Ratings ☆ ☆ ☆ ☆ ☆

Recipe:

Serving:

Prep Time:

Cook Time:

Temperature:

Ingredients:

Methods:

Wine Pairing:

From the Kitchen of:

Wine Name

Winery Region

Grapes Vintage Alcohol %

Appearance		☆ ☆ ☆ ☆ ☆
Aroma		☆ ☆ ☆ ☆ ☆
Body		☆ ☆ ☆ ☆ ☆
Taste		☆ ☆ ☆ ☆ ☆
Finish		☆ ☆ ☆ ☆ ☆

Pairs With

Serving Temperature

Notes

Ratings ☆ ☆ ☆ ☆ ☆

Recipe:

Serving:

Prep Time:

Cook Time:

Temperature:

Ingredients:

Methods:

Wine Pairing:

From the Kitchen of:

Wine Name ______________________

Winery ____________ Region ____________

Grapes ____________ Vintage ____________ Alcohol % ________

Appearance		☆ ☆ ☆ ☆ ☆
Aroma		☆ ☆ ☆ ☆ ☆
Body		☆ ☆ ☆ ☆ ☆
Taste		☆ ☆ ☆ ☆ ☆
Finish		☆ ☆ ☆ ☆ ☆

Pairs With	Serving Temperature

Notes

Ratings ☆ ☆ ☆ ☆ ☆

Recipe:

Serving:

Prep Time:

Cook Time:

Temperature:

Ingredients:

Methods:

Wine Pairing:

From the Kitchen of:

Wine Name

Winery ______ Region ______

Grapes ______ Vintage ______ Alcohol % ______

Appearance		☆ ☆ ☆ ☆ ☆
Aroma		☆ ☆ ☆ ☆ ☆
Body		☆ ☆ ☆ ☆ ☆
Taste		☆ ☆ ☆ ☆ ☆
Finish		☆ ☆ ☆ ☆ ☆

Pairs With	Serving Temperature

Notes

Ratings ☆ ☆ ☆ ☆ ☆

Recipe:

Serving:

Prep Time:

Cook Time:

Temperature:

Ingredients:

Methods:

Wine Pairing:

From the Kitchen of:

Wine Name ______________________

Winery ____________ Region ____________

Grapes ____________ Vintage ____________ Alcohol % ________

Appearance		☆ ☆ ☆ ☆ ☆
Aroma		☆ ☆ ☆ ☆ ☆
Body		☆ ☆ ☆ ☆ ☆
Taste		☆ ☆ ☆ ☆ ☆
Finish		☆ ☆ ☆ ☆ ☆

Pairs With	Serving Temperature

Notes

Ratings ☆ ☆ ☆ ☆ ☆

Recipe:

Serving:

Prep Time:

Cook Time:

Temperature:

Ingredients:

Methods:

Wine Pairing:

From the Kitchen of:

Wine Name ____________________

Winery ____________________ Region ____________________

Grapes ____________________ Vintage ____________________ Alcohol % ____________

Appearance		☆ ☆ ☆ ☆ ☆
Aroma		☆ ☆ ☆ ☆ ☆
Body		☆ ☆ ☆ ☆ ☆
Taste		☆ ☆ ☆ ☆ ☆
Finish		☆ ☆ ☆ ☆ ☆

Pairs With	Serving Temperature

Notes

Ratings ☆ ☆ ☆ ☆ ☆

Recipe:

Serving:

Prep Time:

Cook Time:

Temperature:

Ingredients:

Methods:

Wine Pairing:

From the Kitchen of:

Wine Name

Winery | Region

Grapes | Vintage | Alcohol %

Appearance		☆ ☆ ☆ ☆ ☆
Aroma		☆ ☆ ☆ ☆ ☆
Body		☆ ☆ ☆ ☆ ☆
Taste		☆ ☆ ☆ ☆ ☆
Finish		☆ ☆ ☆ ☆ ☆

Pairs With	Serving Temperature

Notes

Ratings ☆ ☆ ☆ ☆ ☆

Recipe:

Serving:

Prep Time:

Cook Time:

Temperature:

Ingredients:

Methods:

Wine Pairing:

From the Kitchen of:

Wine Name

Winery | Region

Grapes | Vintage | Alcohol %

Appearance		☆ ☆ ☆ ☆ ☆
Aroma		☆ ☆ ☆ ☆ ☆
Body		☆ ☆ ☆ ☆ ☆
Taste		☆ ☆ ☆ ☆ ☆
Finish		☆ ☆ ☆ ☆ ☆

Pairs With	Serving Temperature

Notes

Ratings ☆ ☆ ☆ ☆ ☆

Recipe:

Serving:

Prep Time:

Cook Time:

Temperature:

Ingredients:

Methods:

Wine Pairing:

From the Kitchen of:

Wine Name ____________________

Winery ____________ Region ____________

Grapes ____________ Vintage ____________ Alcohol % ________

Appearance		☆ ☆ ☆ ☆ ☆
Aroma		☆ ☆ ☆ ☆ ☆
Body		☆ ☆ ☆ ☆ ☆
Taste		☆ ☆ ☆ ☆ ☆
Finish		☆ ☆ ☆ ☆ ☆

Pairs With	Serving Temperature

Notes

Ratings ☆ ☆ ☆ ☆ ☆

Recipe:

Serving:

Prep Time:

Cook Time:

Temperature:

Ingredients:

Methods:

Wine Pairing:

From the Kitchen of:

Wine Name

Winery Region

Grapes Vintage Alcohol %

Appearance		☆ ☆ ☆ ☆ ☆
Aroma		☆ ☆ ☆ ☆ ☆
Body		☆ ☆ ☆ ☆ ☆
Taste		☆ ☆ ☆ ☆ ☆
Finish		☆ ☆ ☆ ☆ ☆

Pairs With	Serving Temperature

Notes

Ratings ☆ ☆ ☆ ☆ ☆

Recipe:

Serving:

Prep Time:

Cook Time:

Temperature:

Ingredients:

Methods:

Wine Pairing:

From the Kitchen of:

Wine Name

Winery Region

Grapes Vintage Alcohol %

Appearance		☆ ☆ ☆ ☆ ☆
Aroma		☆ ☆ ☆ ☆ ☆
Body		☆ ☆ ☆ ☆ ☆
Taste		☆ ☆ ☆ ☆ ☆
Finish		☆ ☆ ☆ ☆ ☆

Pairs With	Serving Temperature

Notes

Ratings ☆ ☆ ☆ ☆ ☆

Recipe:

Serving: | Prep Time:

Cook Time: | Temperature:

Ingredients:

Methods:

Wine Pairing:

From the Kitchen of:

Wine Name ____________________

Winery ____________ Region ____________

Grapes ____________ Vintage ____________ Alcohol % ____________

Appearance		☆ ☆ ☆ ☆ ☆
Aroma		☆ ☆ ☆ ☆ ☆
Body		☆ ☆ ☆ ☆ ☆
Taste		☆ ☆ ☆ ☆ ☆
Finish		☆ ☆ ☆ ☆ ☆

Pairs With	Serving Temperature

Notes

Ratings ☆ ☆ ☆ ☆ ☆

Recipe:

Serving:

Prep Time:

Cook Time:

Temperature:

Ingredients:

Methods:

Wine Pairing:

From the Kitchen of:

Wine Name

Winery ____________ Region ____________

Grapes ____________ Vintage ____________ Alcohol % ____________

Appearance		☆ ☆ ☆ ☆ ☆
Aroma		☆ ☆ ☆ ☆ ☆
Body		☆ ☆ ☆ ☆ ☆
Taste		☆ ☆ ☆ ☆ ☆
Finish		☆ ☆ ☆ ☆ ☆

Pairs With	Serving Temperature

Notes

Ratings ☆ ☆ ☆ ☆ ☆

Recipe:

Serving:

Prep Time:

Cook Time:

Temperature:

Ingredients:

Methods:

Wine Pairing:

From the Kitchen of:

Wine Name ____________________

Winery ____________ Region ____________

Grapes ____________ Vintage ____________ Alcohol % ________

Appearance		☆ ☆ ☆ ☆ ☆
Aroma		☆ ☆ ☆ ☆ ☆
Body		☆ ☆ ☆ ☆ ☆
Taste		☆ ☆ ☆ ☆ ☆
Finish		☆ ☆ ☆ ☆ ☆

Pairs With	Serving Temperature

Notes

Ratings ☆ ☆ ☆ ☆ ☆

Recipe:

Serving:

Prep Time:

Cook Time:

Temperature:

Ingredients:

Methods:

Wine Pairing:

From the Kitchen of:

Wine Name ______________________

Winery ______________ Region ______________

Grapes ______________ Vintage ______________ Alcohol % __________

Appearance		☆ ☆ ☆ ☆ ☆
Aroma		☆ ☆ ☆ ☆ ☆
Body		☆ ☆ ☆ ☆ ☆
Taste		☆ ☆ ☆ ☆ ☆
Finish		☆ ☆ ☆ ☆ ☆

Pairs With	Serving Temperature

Notes

Ratings ☆ ☆ ☆ ☆ ☆

Recipe:

Serving:

Prep Time:

Cook Time:

Temperature:

Ingredients:

Methods:

Wine Pairing:

From the Kitchen of:

Wine Name

Winery Region

Grapes Vintage Alcohol %

Appearance		☆ ☆ ☆ ☆ ☆
Aroma		☆ ☆ ☆ ☆ ☆
Body		☆ ☆ ☆ ☆ ☆
Taste		☆ ☆ ☆ ☆ ☆
Finish		☆ ☆ ☆ ☆ ☆

Pairs With

Serving Temperature

Notes

Ratings ☆ ☆ ☆ ☆ ☆

Recipe:

Serving:

Prep Time:

Cook Time:

Temperature:

Ingredients:

Methods:

Wine Pairing:

From the Kitchen of:

Wine Name

Winery | Region

Grapes | Vintage | Alcohol %

Appearance		☆ ☆ ☆ ☆ ☆
Aroma		☆ ☆ ☆ ☆ ☆
Body		☆ ☆ ☆ ☆ ☆
Taste		☆ ☆ ☆ ☆ ☆
Finish		☆ ☆ ☆ ☆ ☆

Pairs With	Serving Temperature

Notes

Ratings ☆ ☆ ☆ ☆ ☆

Recipe:

Serving:

Prep Time:

Cook Time:

Temperature:

Ingredients:

Methods:

Wine Pairing:

From the Kitchen of:

Wine Name

Winery Region

Grapes Vintage Alcohol %

Appearance		☆ ☆ ☆ ☆ ☆
Aroma		☆ ☆ ☆ ☆ ☆
Body		☆ ☆ ☆ ☆ ☆
Taste		☆ ☆ ☆ ☆ ☆
Finish		☆ ☆ ☆ ☆ ☆

Pairs With

Serving Temperature

Notes

Ratings ☆ ☆ ☆ ☆ ☆

Recipe:

Serving:

Prep Time:

Cook Time:

Temperature:

Ingredients:

Methods:

Wine Pairing:

From the Kitchen of:

Wine Name

Winery | Region

Grapes | Vintage | Alcohol %

Appearance		☆ ☆ ☆ ☆ ☆
Aroma		☆ ☆ ☆ ☆ ☆
Body		☆ ☆ ☆ ☆ ☆
Taste		☆ ☆ ☆ ☆ ☆
Finish		☆ ☆ ☆ ☆ ☆

Pairs With	Serving Temperature

Notes

Ratings ☆ ☆ ☆ ☆ ☆

Recipe:

Serving:

Prep Time:

Cook Time:

Temperature:

Ingredients:

Methods:

Wine Pairing:

From the Kitchen of:

Wine Name

Winery ____________ Region ____________

Grapes ____________ Vintage ____________ Alcohol % ____________

Appearance		☆ ☆ ☆ ☆ ☆
Aroma		☆ ☆ ☆ ☆ ☆
Body		☆ ☆ ☆ ☆ ☆
Taste		☆ ☆ ☆ ☆ ☆
Finish		☆ ☆ ☆ ☆ ☆

Pairs With	Serving Temperature

Notes

Ratings ☆ ☆ ☆ ☆ ☆

Recipe:

Serving:

Prep Time:

Cook Time:

Temperature:

Ingredients:

Methods:

Wine Pairing:

From the Kitchen of:

Wine Name

Winery Region

Grapes Vintage Alcohol %

Appearance		☆ ☆ ☆ ☆ ☆
Aroma		☆ ☆ ☆ ☆ ☆
Body		☆ ☆ ☆ ☆ ☆
Taste		☆ ☆ ☆ ☆ ☆
Finish		☆ ☆ ☆ ☆ ☆

Pairs With	Serving Temperature

Notes

Ratings ☆ ☆ ☆ ☆ ☆

Recipe:

Serving:

Prep Time:

Cook Time:

Temperature:

Ingredients:

Methods:

Wine Pairing:

From the Kitchen of:

Wine Name

Winery Region

Grapes Vintage Alcohol %

Appearance		☆ ☆ ☆ ☆ ☆
Aroma		☆ ☆ ☆ ☆ ☆
Body		☆ ☆ ☆ ☆ ☆
Taste		☆ ☆ ☆ ☆ ☆
Finish		☆ ☆ ☆ ☆ ☆

Pairs With	Serving Temperature

Notes

Ratings ☆ ☆ ☆ ☆ ☆

Recipe:

Serving:

Prep Time:

Cook Time:

Temperature:

Ingredients:

Methods:

Wine Pairing:

From the Kitchen of:

Wine Name

Winery ____________ Region ____________

Grapes ____________ Vintage ____________ Alcohol % ____________

Appearance		☆ ☆ ☆ ☆ ☆
Aroma		☆ ☆ ☆ ☆ ☆
Body		☆ ☆ ☆ ☆ ☆
Taste		☆ ☆ ☆ ☆ ☆
Finish		☆ ☆ ☆ ☆ ☆

Pairs With	Serving Temperature

Notes

Ratings ☆ ☆ ☆ ☆ ☆

Recipe:

Serving:

Prep Time:

Cook Time:

Temperature:

Ingredients:

Methods:

Wine Pairing:

From the Kitchen of:

Wine Name ____________________

Winery ____________ Region ____________

Grapes ____________ Vintage ____________ Alcohol % ________

Appearance		☆ ☆ ☆ ☆ ☆
Aroma		☆ ☆ ☆ ☆ ☆
Body		☆ ☆ ☆ ☆ ☆
Taste		☆ ☆ ☆ ☆ ☆
Finish		☆ ☆ ☆ ☆ ☆

Pairs With	Serving Temperature

Notes

Ratings ☆ ☆ ☆ ☆ ☆

Recipe:

Serving:

Prep Time:

Cook Time:

Temperature:

Ingredients:

Methods:

Wine Pairing:

From the Kitchen of:

Wine Name

Winery ____________ Region ____________

Grapes ____________ Vintage ____________ Alcohol % ____________

Appearance		☆ ☆ ☆ ☆ ☆
Aroma		☆ ☆ ☆ ☆ ☆
Body		☆ ☆ ☆ ☆ ☆
Taste		☆ ☆ ☆ ☆ ☆
Finish		☆ ☆ ☆ ☆ ☆

Pairs With	Serving Temperature

Notes

Ratings ☆ ☆ ☆ ☆ ☆

Recipe:

Serving:

Prep Time:

Cook Time:

Temperature:

Ingredients:

Methods:

Wine Pairing:

From the Kitchen of:

Wine Name

Winery ______ Region ______

Grapes ______ Vintage ______ Alcohol % ______

Appearance		☆ ☆ ☆ ☆ ☆
Aroma		☆ ☆ ☆ ☆ ☆
Body		☆ ☆ ☆ ☆ ☆
Taste		☆ ☆ ☆ ☆ ☆
Finish		☆ ☆ ☆ ☆ ☆

Pairs With	Serving Temperature

Notes

Ratings ☆ ☆ ☆ ☆ ☆

Recipe:

Serving:

Prep Time:

Cook Time:

Temperature:

Ingredients:

Methods:

Wine Pairing:

From the Kitchen of:

Wine Name

Winery Region

Grapes Vintage Alcohol %

Appearance		☆ ☆ ☆ ☆ ☆
Aroma		☆ ☆ ☆ ☆ ☆
Body		☆ ☆ ☆ ☆ ☆
Taste		☆ ☆ ☆ ☆ ☆
Finish		☆ ☆ ☆ ☆ ☆

Pairs With	Serving Temperature

Notes

Ratings ☆ ☆ ☆ ☆ ☆

Recipe:

Serving:

Prep Time:

Cook Time:

Temperature:

Ingredients:

Methods:

Wine Pairing:

From the Kitchen of:

Wine Name ____________________

Winery ____________ Region ____________

Grapes ____________ Vintage ____________ Alcohol % ________

Appearance		☆ ☆ ☆ ☆ ☆
Aroma		☆ ☆ ☆ ☆ ☆
Body		☆ ☆ ☆ ☆ ☆
Taste		☆ ☆ ☆ ☆ ☆
Finish		☆ ☆ ☆ ☆ ☆

Pairs With	Serving Temperature

Notes

Ratings ☆ ☆ ☆ ☆ ☆

Recipe:

Serving:

Prep Time:

Cook Time:

Temperature:

Ingredients:

Methods:

Wine Pairing:

From the Kitchen of:

Wine Name

Winery Region

Grapes Vintage Alcohol %

Appearance		☆ ☆ ☆ ☆ ☆
Aroma		☆ ☆ ☆ ☆ ☆
Body		☆ ☆ ☆ ☆ ☆
Taste		☆ ☆ ☆ ☆ ☆
Finish		☆ ☆ ☆ ☆ ☆

Pairs With	Serving Temperature

Notes

Ratings ☆ ☆ ☆ ☆ ☆

Recipe:

Serving:

Prep Time:

Cook Time:

Temperature:

Ingredients:

Methods:

Wine Pairing:

From the Kitchen of:

Wine Name

Winery Region

Grapes Vintage Alcohol %

Appearance		☆ ☆ ☆ ☆ ☆
Aroma		☆ ☆ ☆ ☆ ☆
Body		☆ ☆ ☆ ☆ ☆
Taste		☆ ☆ ☆ ☆ ☆
Finish		☆ ☆ ☆ ☆ ☆

Pairs With	Serving Temperature

Notes

Ratings ☆ ☆ ☆ ☆ ☆

Recipe:

Serving:

Prep Time:

Cook Time:

Temperature:

Ingredients:

Methods:

Wine Pairing:

From the Kitchen of:

Wine Name

Winery Region

Grapes Vintage Alcohol %

Appearance		☆ ☆ ☆ ☆ ☆
Aroma		☆ ☆ ☆ ☆ ☆
Body		☆ ☆ ☆ ☆ ☆
Taste		☆ ☆ ☆ ☆ ☆
Finish		☆ ☆ ☆ ☆ ☆

Pairs With	Serving Temperature

Notes

Ratings ☆ ☆ ☆ ☆ ☆

Recipe:

Serving:

Prep Time:

Cook Time:

Temperature:

Ingredients:

Methods:

Wine Pairing:

From the Kitchen of:

Wine Name

Winery Region

Grapes Vintage Alcohol %

Appearance		☆ ☆ ☆ ☆ ☆
Aroma		☆ ☆ ☆ ☆ ☆
Body		☆ ☆ ☆ ☆ ☆
Taste		☆ ☆ ☆ ☆ ☆
Finish		☆ ☆ ☆ ☆ ☆

Pairs With

Serving Temperature

Notes

Ratings ☆ ☆ ☆ ☆ ☆

Recipe:

Serving:

Prep Time:

Cook Time:

Temperature:

Ingredients:

Methods:

Wine Pairing:

From the Kitchen of:

Wine Name

Winery ________ Region ________

Grapes ________ Vintage ________ Alcohol % ________

Appearance		☆ ☆ ☆ ☆ ☆
Aroma		☆ ☆ ☆ ☆ ☆
Body		☆ ☆ ☆ ☆ ☆
Taste		☆ ☆ ☆ ☆ ☆
Finish		☆ ☆ ☆ ☆ ☆

Pairs With	Serving Temperature

Notes

Ratings ☆ ☆ ☆ ☆ ☆

Recipe:

Serving:

Prep Time:

Cook Time:

Temperature:

Ingredients:

Methods:

Wine Pairing:

From the Kitchen of:

Wine Name ______________________

Winery ______________ Region ______________

Grapes ______________ Vintage ______________ Alcohol % ________

Appearance		☆ ☆ ☆ ☆ ☆
Aroma		☆ ☆ ☆ ☆ ☆
Body		☆ ☆ ☆ ☆ ☆
Taste		☆ ☆ ☆ ☆ ☆
Finish		☆ ☆ ☆ ☆ ☆

Pairs With	Serving Temperature

Notes

Ratings ☆ ☆ ☆ ☆ ☆

Recipe:

Serving:

Prep Time:

Cook Time:

Temperature:

Ingredients:

Methods:

Wine Pairing:

From the Kitchen of:

Wine Name

Winery Region

Grapes Vintage Alcohol %

Appearance		☆ ☆ ☆ ☆ ☆
Aroma		☆ ☆ ☆ ☆ ☆
Body		☆ ☆ ☆ ☆ ☆
Taste		☆ ☆ ☆ ☆ ☆
Finish		☆ ☆ ☆ ☆ ☆

Pairs With	Serving Temperature

Notes

Ratings ☆ ☆ ☆ ☆ ☆

Recipe:

Serving:

Prep Time:

Cook Time:

Temperature:

Ingredients:

Methods:

Wine Pairing:

From the Kitchen of:

Wine Name

Winery | Region

Grapes | Vintage | Alcohol %

Appearance		☆ ☆ ☆ ☆ ☆
Aroma		☆ ☆ ☆ ☆ ☆
Body		☆ ☆ ☆ ☆ ☆
Taste		☆ ☆ ☆ ☆ ☆
Finish		☆ ☆ ☆ ☆ ☆

Pairs With	Serving Temperature

Notes

Ratings ☆ ☆ ☆ ☆ ☆

Made in the USA
Las Vegas, NV
25 March 2022

46275427R00057